FOR THE BEST SISTER IN THE WORLD

summersdale

FOR THE BEST SISTER IN THE WORLD

Text compiled by Elanor Clarke

Summersdale Publishers Ltd
46 West Street
Chichester
West Sussex
PO19 1RP
UK

www.summersdale.com

Printed and bound in the Czech Republic

ISBN: 978-1-84953-668-4

Substantial discounts on bulk quantities of Summersdale books are available to corporations, professional associations and other organisations. For details contact Nicky Douglas by telephone: +44 (0) 1243 756902, fax: +44 (0) 1243 786300 or email: nicky@summersdale.com.

A little something
from me to you.
♡

TO Kimberley

FROM Jessie x x x x x

A SISTER IS A GIFT TO
THE HEART, A FRIEND
TO THE SPIRIT, A
GOLDEN THREAD TO THE
MEANING OF LIFE.

Isadora James

WHATEVER YOU DO THEY WILL LOVE YOU.

Deborah Moggach on sisters

IS SOLACE ANYWHERE MORE COMFORTING THAN THAT IN THE ARMS OF A SISTER?

Alice Walker

A LOVING HEART WAS
BETTER AND STRONGER
THAN WISDOM.

Charles Dickens

I SUSTAIN MYSELF
WITH THE LOVE
OF FAMILY.

Maya Angelou

BROTHERS AND SISTERS NEVER FAIL TO SEE THE BEST IN EACH OTHER.

Gregory E. Lang

I WOULD LIKE MORE
SISTERS, THAT THE
TAKING OUT OF ONE,
MIGHT NOT LEAVE
SUCH STILLNESS.

Emily Dickinson

TO HELP ONE ANOTHER IS PART OF THE RELIGION OF OUR SISTERHOOD.

Louisa May Alcott

ARE WE NOT
LIKE TWO VOLUMES
OF ONE BOOK?

Marceline Desbordes-Valmore

SISTER, AWAKE!
CLOSE NOT YOUR EYES!
THE DAY HER LIGHT
DISCLOSES,
AND THE BRIGHT
MORNING DOTH ARISE
OUT OF HER BED
OF ROSES.

Thomas Bateson

IN THEE MY SOUL SHALL
OWN COMBINED THE
SISTER AND THE FRIEND.

Catherine Killigrew

BROTHERS AND SISTERS ARE AS CLOSE AS HANDS AND FEET.

Vietnamese proverb

FRIENDS MAY
COME AND GO,
BUT SISTERS ARE
FOREVER

A SISTER CAN BE SEEN
AS SOMEONE WHO
IS BOTH OURSELVES
AND VERY MUCH NOT
OURSELVES – A SPECIAL
KIND OF DOUBLE.

Toni Morrison

CHILDREN OF THE SAME
FAMILY, THE SAME
BLOOD, WITH THE SAME
FIRST ASSOCIATIONS
AND HABITS, HAVE SOME
MEANS OF ENJOYMENT
IN THEIR POWER,
WHICH NO SUBSEQUENT
CONNECTIONS CAN SUPPLY.

Jane Austen

HAVING A PLACE TO GO
~ IS A HOME. HAVING
SOMEONE TO LOVE ~ IS A
FAMILY. HAVING BOTH ~
IS A BLESSING.

Donna Hedges

REJOICE WITH
YOUR FAMILY IN THE
BEAUTIFUL LAND
OF LIFE!

Albert Einstein

PROBABLY THE
MOST COMPETITIVE
RELATIONSHIP WITHIN
THE FAMILY, BUT ONCE
THE SISTERS ARE
GROWN, IT BECOMES
THE STRONGEST
RELATIONSHIP.

Margaret Mead on sisterhood

BLESS YOU, MY DARLING,
AND REMEMBER YOU ARE
ALWAYS IN THE HEART...
OF YOUR SISTER.

Katherine Mansfield

A HAPPY FAMILY IS BUT AN EARLIER HEAVEN.

George Bernard Shaw

A SISTER SMILES WHEN
ONE TELLS ONE'S STORIES
— FOR SHE KNOWS WHERE
THE DECORATION HAS
BEEN ADDED.

Chris Montaigne

THERE IS GREAT COMFORT
AND INSPIRATION IN
THE FEELING OF CLOSE
HUMAN RELATIONSHIPS
AND ITS BEARING ON OUR
MUTUAL FORTUNES.

Walt Disney

MORE THAN SANTA
CLAUS, YOUR SISTER
KNOWS WHEN YOU'VE
BEEN BAD AND GOOD.

Linda Sunshine

I, WHO HAVE NO SISTERS
OR BROTHERS, LOOK
WITH SOME DEGREE
OF INNOCENT ENVY ON
THOSE WHO MAY BE SAID
TO BE BORN TO FRIENDS.

James Boswell

OTHER THINGS
MAY CHANGE US, BUT
WE START AND END
WITH FAMILY.

Anthony Brandt

HOW DO PEOPLE MAKE IT THROUGH LIFE WITHOUT A SISTER?

Sara Corpening Whiteford

OUR MOST BASIC
INSTINCT IS NOT
FOR SURVIVAL BUT
FOR FAMILY.

Paul Pearsall

KNOWING I
HAVE A SISTER,
I KNOW I ALWAYS
HAVE A FRIEND

FAMILY IS WHAT
GROUNDS YOU.

Angelina Jolie

THERE CAN BE NO
SITUATION IN LIFE
IN WHICH THE
CONVERSATION OF MY
DEAR SISTER WILL
NOT ADMINISTER SOME
COMFORT TO ME.

Mary Wortley Montagu

THE VOICE, O TENDER
VOICES, MEMORY'S
LOVING VOICES!
LAST MIRACLE OF ALL,
O DEAREST MOTHER'S,
SISTER'S, VOICES.

Walt Whitman

LOVE IS THE CONDITION
IN WHICH THE HAPPINESS
OF ANOTHER PERSON IS
ESSENTIAL TO YOUR OWN.

Robert A. Heinlein

A SISTER IS BOTH
YOUR MIRROR AND
YOUR OPPOSITE.

Elizabeth Fishel

MOST ARE LIKE MY
SISTER AND ME... LINKED
BY VOLATILE LOVE, BEST
FRIENDS WHO MAKE
OTHER BEST FRIENDS...
SLIGHTLY LESS BEST.

Patricia Volk

SISTERLY LOVE IS, OF
ALL SENTIMENTS, THE
MOST ABSTRACT.

Ugo Betti

THE FAMILY — THAT DEAR
OCTOPUS FROM WHOSE
TENTACLES WE NEVER
QUITE ESCAPE, NOR, IN
OUR INMOST HEARTS,
EVER QUITE WISH TO.

Dodie Smith

IF YOU ONLY HAVE ONE
SMILE IN YOU, GIVE IT TO
THE PEOPLE YOU LOVE.

Maya Angelou

SWEET IS THE VOICE OF
A SISTER IN THE SEASON
OF SORROW, AND WISE IS
THE COUNSEL OF THOSE
WHO LOVE US.

Benjamin Disraeli

OH! PLEASANT, PLEASANT
WERE THE DAYS,
THE TIME, WHEN, IN OUR
CHILDISH PLAYS,
MY SISTER... AND I
TOGETHER CHASED
THE BUTTERFLY!

William Wordsworth

A SISTER IS LIKE HAVING
A BEST FRIEND YOU CAN'T
GET RID OF... WHATEVER
YOU DO, THEY'LL STILL
BE THERE.

Amy Li

THE BEST THING
ABOUT HAVING A SISTER
WAS THAT I ALWAYS
HAD A FRIEND.

Cali Rae Turner

THE FAMILY
IS THE COUNTRY
OF THE HEART.

Giuseppe Mazzini

AN OLDER SISTER HELPS
ONE REMAIN HALF
CHILD, HALF WOMAN.

Anonymous

SISTERS ARE THERE
WITH US FROM THE
DAWN OF OUR PERSONAL
STORIES TO THE
INEVITABLE DUSK.

Susan Scarf Merrell

YOU KNOW ALL
MY SECRETS AND
STILL LOVE ME

IN TIME OF TEST, FAMILY IS BEST.

Burmese proverb

SISTERS FUNCTION
AS SAFETY NETS IN A
CHAOTIC WORLD SIMPLY
BY BEING THERE FOR
EACH OTHER.

Carol Saline

YOU DON'T CHOOSE
YOUR FAMILY. THEY ARE
GOD'S GIFT TO YOU, AS
YOU ARE TO THEM.

Desmond Tutu

I DON'T BELIEVE AN
ACCIDENT OF BIRTH
MAKES PEOPLE SISTERS...
SISTERHOOD... IS A
CONDITION PEOPLE HAVE
TO WORK AT.

Maya Angelou

CHERISH YOUR FAMILY,
MAKE TIME, HAVE
PATIENCE, AND LAUGH
OFTEN WITH THEM.

Anonymous

A SIBLING MAY
BE THE KEEPER OF
ONE'S IDENTITY, THE
ONLY PERSON WITH
THE KEYS TO ONE'S
UNFETTERED, MORE
FUNDAMENTAL SELF.

Marian Sandmaier

FAMILY TRADITIONS...
HELP US DEFINE WHO
WE ARE; THEY PROVIDE
SOMETHING STEADY,
RELIABLE AND SAFE IN A
CONFUSING WORLD.

Susan Lieberman

IN FAMILY LIFE,
LOVE IS THE OIL THAT
EASES FRICTION, THE
CEMENT THAT BINDS...
AND THE MUSIC THAT
BRINGS HARMONY.

Eva Burrows

YOU ALWAYS
KNOW THE RIGHT
THING TO SAY

A SISTER SHARES
CHILDHOOD MEMORIES
AND GROWN-UP DREAMS.

Anonymous

LOVE IS THE STRONGEST
FORCE THE WORLD
POSSESSES.

Mahatma Gandhi

A WOMAN COULD BOTH
LOVE HER SISTER
DEARLY AND WANT TO
WRING HER NECK AT
THE SAME TIME.

Linda Sunshine

SISTERHOOD IS POWERFUL.

Robin Morgan

IF THE FAMILY WERE
A FRUIT, IT WOULD
BE AN ORANGE, A
CIRCLE OF SECTIONS,
HELD TOGETHER BUT
SEPARABLE — EACH
SEGMENT DISTINCT.

Letty Cottin Pogrebin

A SISTER IS A
FOREVER FRIEND.

Anonymous

WE ACQUIRE FRIENDS
AND WE MAKE ENEMIES,
BUT OUR SISTERS COME
WITH THE TERRITORY.

Evelyn Loeb

SISTERS ARE
BLOSSOMS IN THE
GARDEN OF LIFE.

Anonymous

THERE IS ONLY ONE HAPPINESS IN LIFE; TO LOVE AND TO BE LOVED.

George Sand

YOU KEEP YOUR PAST
BY HAVING SISTERS...
THEY'RE THE ONLY ONES
WHO DON'T GET BORED
IF YOU TALK ABOUT
YOUR MEMORIES.

Deborah Moggach

BELOVED, YOU ARE MY
SISTER... YOU ARE MY
FACE; YOU ARE ME.

Toni Morrison

SHE IS YOUR MIRROR,
SHINING BACK AT YOU
WITH A WORLD OF
POSSIBILITIES.

Barbara Alpert

SISTERS... ARE
PEOPLE WITH WHOM
YOU CAN TALK WITH
ABOUT ANYTHING.

Catherine Pulsifer

IT WAS NICE GROWING UP
WITH SOMEONE LIKE YOU
— SOMEONE TO LEAN ON,
SOMEONE TO COUNT ON...
SOMEONE TO TELL ON!

Anonymous

WE HAVE BEEN BANDED
TOGETHER UNDER PACK
CODES AND TRIBAL LAWS.

Rose Macaulay

FOR THERE IS NO FRIEND
LIKE A SISTER, IN CALM
OR STORMY WEATHER, TO
CHEER ONE ON THE TEDIOUS
WAY, TO FETCH ONE IF ONE
GOES ASTRAY, TO LIFT ONE
IF ONE TOTTERS DOWN, TO
STRENGTHEN WHILST
ONE STANDS.

Christina Rossetti

YOU'RE ALWAYS
THERE WHEN I
NEED YOU

WHAT SETS SISTERS
APART FROM BROTHERS
IS A VERY INTIMATE
MESHING OF HEART,
SOUL AND THE MYSTICAL
CORDS OF MEMORY.

Carol Saline

TO HAVE A LOVING
RELATIONSHIP WITH A
SISTER IS... TO HAVE A
SOULMATE FOR LIFE.

Victoria Secunda

SISTERS ARE CONNECTED
THROUGHOUT THEIR
LIVES BY A SPECIAL
BOND... SISTERS REMAIN
SISTERS, UNTIL DEATH
DO THEM PART.

Brigid McConville

OUR SISTERS HOLD UP
OUR MIRRORS: OUR
IMAGES OF WHO WE
ARE AND WHO WE CAN
DARE TO BECOME.

Elizabeth Fishel

A SISTER IS A FRIEND
YOU DON'T HAVE TO
AVOID THE TRUTH WITH.

Michelle Malm

NO ONE KNOWS BETTER THAN A SISTER HOW WE GREW UP.

Dale V. Atkins

OH, THE COMFORT...
HAVING NEITHER TO
WEIGH THOUGHTS NOR
MEASURE WORDS, BUT
POURING THEM ALL
RIGHT OUT, JUST AS
THEY ARE.

Dinah Craik

A SISTER WILL ALWAYS NOTICE HER SISTER'S FIRST GREY HAIRS WITH GLEE.

Allison M. Lee

THERE IS SPACE
WITHIN SISTERHOOD
FOR LIKENESS
AND DIFFERENCE...
THERE IS SPACE FOR
DISAPPOINTMENT AND
SURPRISE.

Christine Downing

LOVE MAKES A FAMILY.

Gigi Kaeser

YOU KNOW FULL WELL
AS I DO THE VALUE OF
SISTERS' AFFECTIONS:
THERE IS NOTHING LIKE
IT IN THIS WORLD.

Charlotte Brontë

SISTERHOOD... IS, LIKE
MOTHERHOOD, A CAPACITY,
NOT A DESTINY. IT MUST
BE CHOSEN, EXERCISED
BY ACTS OF WILL.

Olga Broumas

ONE'S SISTER IS PART OF
ONE'S ESSENTIAL SELF,
AN ETERNAL PRESENCE
OF ONE'S HEART AND
SOUL AND MEMORY.

Susan Cabill

EVEN THOUGH I CAN'T
SOLVE YOUR PROBLEMS,
I WILL BE THERE AS
YOUR SOUNDING BOARD
WHENEVER YOU
NEED ME.

Sandra K. Lamberson

YOU ARE
THE BEST!

SISTERS BECOME MORE
BEAUTIFUL AS EACH
DAY PASSES BY.

Michelle Malm

IN EVERY CONCEIVABLE
MANNER, THE FAMILY
IS LINK TO OUR PAST,
BRIDGE TO OUR FUTURE.

Alex Haley

IN THE COOKIES OF
LIFE, SISTERS ARE THE
CHOCOLATE CHIPS.

Anonymous

WE ARE SISTERS. WE
WILL ALWAYS BE SISTERS.
OUR DIFFERENCES MAY
NEVER GO AWAY BUT
NEITHER, FOR ME,
WILL OUR SONG.

Elizabeth Fishel

MY SISTER
ACCOMMODATES ME...
SHE ACCEPTS AND
LOVES ME, DESPITE OUR
DIFFERENCES.

Joy Harjo

MY FIRST JOB IS BIG
SISTER AND I TAKE THAT
VERY SERIOUSLY.

Venus Williams

AN OUNCE OF BLOOD IS WORTH MORE THAN A POUND OF FRIENDSHIP.

Spanish proverb

MY SIBLINGS ARE MY
BEST FRIENDS.

America Ferrera

OUR DAYS OUT
TOGETHER ARE
THE MOST FUN!

LIKE BRANCHES
ON A TREE WE GROW
IN DIFFERENT
DIRECTIONS YET OUR
ROOTS REMAIN AS ONE.

Anonymous

SIBLINGS: CHILDREN OF
THE SAME PARENTS, EACH
OF WHOM IS PERFECTLY
NORMAL UNTIL THEY
GET TOGETHER.

Sam Levenson

A FAMILY NEEDS TO
WORK AS A TEAM,
SUPPORTING EACH
OTHER'S INDIVIDUAL
AIMS AND ASPIRATIONS.

Buzz Aldrin

YOUR SIBLINGS ARE
THE ONLY PEOPLE... WHO
KNOW WHAT IT'S LIKE TO
HAVE BEEN BROUGHT UP
THE WAY YOU WERE.

Betsy Cohen

A MINISTERING ANGEL SHALL MY SISTER BE.

William Shakespeare

YOU CAN'T THINK HOW
I DEPEND ON YOU, AND
WHEN YOU'RE NOT
THERE THE COLOUR
GOES OUT OF MY LIFE.

Virginia Woolf in a letter
to her sister

THE FAMILY IS ONE OF NATURE'S MASTERPIECES.

George Santayana

A LOYAL SISTER
IS WORTH A
THOUSAND FRIENDS.

Marian Eigerman

ONE REFUSING A SIBLING'S ADVICE BREAKS HIS ARM.

Somali proverb

BE WHO YOU ARE
AND SAY WHAT YOU FEEL
BECAUSE THOSE WHO
MIND DON'T MATTER
AND THOSE WHO MATTER
DON'T MIND.

Dr Seuss

YOU HELP ME
KNOW WHO I
REALLY AM

THE BOND THAT LINKS
YOUR TRUE FAMILY
IS NOT ONE OF BLOOD,
BUT OF... JOY IN EACH
OTHER'S LIFE.

Richard Bach

A TRUE SISTER IS A
FRIEND WHO LISTENS
WITH HER HEART.

Anonymous

WHEN MUM AND DAD
DON'T UNDERSTAND, A
SISTER ALWAYS WILL.

Anonymous

A FAMILY IN HARMONY WILL PROSPER IN EVERYTHING.

Chinese proverb

SHE IS YOUR WITNESS,
WHO SEES YOU AT YOUR
WORST AND BEST AND
LOVES YOU ANYWAY.

Barbara Alpert

THERE IS NO DOUBT
THAT IT IS AROUND THE
FAMILY AND THE HOME
THAT ALL THE GREATEST
VIRTUES... ARE CREATED,
STRENGTHENED AND
MAINTAINED.

Winston Churchill

FAMILIES ARE
THE BEST PLACE TO
LEARN AND PRACTISE
MUTUAL TOLERANCE
AND ACCEPTANCE.

Inaara Aga Khan

BIG SISTERS ARE THE
CRAB GRASS IN THE
LAWN OF LIFE.

Charles M. Schulz

IF I COULD
CHOOSE MY
FAMILY, I'D STILL
CHOOSE YOU

SHE IS MY SOUNDING
BOARD, MY CONFIDANTE,
MY KEEPER OF SECRETS
— AND MY BEST FRIEND.

Kathleen O'Keefe

FAMILY FACES ARE
MAGIC MIRRORS.
LOOKING AT PEOPLE WHO
BELONG TO US, WE SEE
THE PAST, PRESENT
AND FUTURE.

Gail Lumet Buckley

SISTER TO SISTER
WE WILL ALWAYS BE,
A COUPLE OF NUTS OFF
THE FAMILY TREE.

Anonymous

PEOPLE COME AND
GO IN OUR LIVES,
BUT OUR FAMILY ARE
ALWAYS THERE.

Catherine Pulsifer

THEN COME, MY SISTER!
COME, I PRAY,
WITH SPEED PUT ON
YOUR WOODLAND DRESS;
AND BRING NO BOOK:
FOR THIS ONE DAY
WE'LL GIVE TO
IDLENESS.

William Wordsworth

YOUR FAMILY AND
YOUR LOVE MUST BE
CULTIVATED LIKE A
GARDEN... TO KEEP
ANY RELATIONSHIP
FLOURISHING AND
GROWING.

Jim Rohn

SISTERS ARE DIFFERENT FLOWERS FROM THE SAME GARDEN.

Anonymous

THE ONLY PEOPLE WHO TRULY KNOW YOUR STORY ARE THE ONES WHO HELP YOU WRITE IT.

Anonymous

I KNOW OUR
FIGHTS WILL
NEVER LAST

OUR SIBLINGS...
RESEMBLE US JUST
ENOUGH TO MAKE ALL
THEIR DIFFERENCES
CONFUSING... WE ARE
CAST IN RELATION TO
THEM OUR WHOLE LIVES.

Susan Scarf Merrell

FAMILIES... HUMANISE
YOU. THEY ARE MADE
TO MAKE YOU FORGET
YOURSELF OCCASIONALLY,
SO THAT THE BEAUTIFUL
BALANCE OF LIFE IS
NOT DESTROYED.

Anaïs Nin

I SMILE BECAUSE
YOU'RE MY SISTER.
I LAUGH BECAUSE
THERE'S NOTHING YOU
CAN DO ABOUT IT.

Anonymous

WE CANNOT DESTROY
KINDRED: OUR CHAINS
STRETCH A LITTLE
SOMETIMES, BUT THEY
NEVER BREAK.

Marquise de Sévigné

TO EACH OTHER, WE
WERE AS NORMAL AND
NICE AS THE SMELL OF
BREAD. WE WERE JUST
A FAMILY.

John Irving

YOU CAN BE BORING AND
TEDIOUS WITH SISTERS,
WHEREAS YOU HAVE TO
PUT ON A GOOD FACE
WITH FRIENDS.

Deborah Moggach

OUR ROOTS SAY WE'RE
SISTERS, OUR HEARTS
SAY WE'RE FRIENDS.

Anonymous

FAMILY LIFE IS TOO
INTIMATE TO BE
PRESERVED BY THE
SPIRIT OF JUSTICE. IT
CAN BE SUSTAINED BY
A SPIRIT OF LOVE.

Reinhold Niebuhr

YOU'RE MY
BEST FRIEND

SISTERS ARE FOR
SHARING LAUGHTER
AND WIPING TEARS.

Anonymous

THE INFORMALITY
OF FAMILY LIFE IS A
BLESSED CONDITION
THAT ALLOWS US ALL TO
BECOME OUR BEST WHILE
LOOKING OUR WORST.

Marge Kennedy

THERE IS NO
BETTER FRIEND THAN
A SISTER AND THERE
IS NO BETTER SISTER
THAN YOU.

Anonymous

LOVE, LIKE A RIVER,
WILL CUT A NEW PATH
WHENEVER IT MEETS
AN OBSTACLE.

Crystal Middlemas

A SISTER IS ONE WHO
REACHES FOR YOUR
HAND AND TOUCHES
YOUR HEART.

Anonymous

MY SISTER TAUGHT ME
EVERYTHING I REALLY
NEED TO KNOW, AND
SHE WAS ONLY IN SIXTH
GRADE AT THE TIME.

Linda Sunshine

THERE IS AN
INTERCONNECTEDNESS
AMONG MEMBERS THAT
BONDS THE FAMILY,
MUCH LIKE MOUNTAIN
CLIMBERS WHO ROPE
THEMSELVES TOGETHER
WHEN CLIMBING.

Phil McGraw

FAMILY LIFE...
ETCHES ITSELF
INTO MEMORY AND
PERSONALITY. IT'S
DIFFICULT TO IMAGINE
ANYTHING MORE
NOURISHING TO
THE SOUL.

Thomas Moore

A SISTER WILL ALWAYS BE AROUND.

Jane Dowdeswell

FAMILY IS THE MOST IMPORTANT THING IN THE WORLD.

Diana, Princess of Wales

SIBLING RELATIONSHIPS...
FLOURISH IN A
THOUSAND INCARNATIONS
OF CLOSENESS AND
DISTANCE, WARMTH,
LOYALTY AND DISTRUST.

Erica E. Goode

THE STRENGTH OF
A FAMILY, LIKE THE
STRENGTH OF AN ARMY,
IS IN ITS LOYALTY TO
EACH OTHER.

Mario Puzo

A SISTER IS ALWAYS
THERE TO DEFEND YOU
NO MATTER WHAT.

Felicity Martin

THERE IS NO TIME LIKE
THE OLD TIME, WHEN
YOU AND I WERE YOUNG!

Oliver Wendell Holmes Sr

LOVE IS ALL WE HAVE,
THE ONLY WAY THAT
EACH CAN HELP
THE OTHER.

Euripides

SISTERS ARE
INESCAPABLY CONNECTED,
SHAPED BY THE SAME
TWO PARENTS, THE SAME
TROVE OF MEMORY AND
EXPERIENCE.

Roxanne Brown

I KNOW I CAN
SHARE ANYTHING
WITH YOU

WHAT GREATER THING
IS THERE FOR TWO
HUMAN SOULS THAN TO
FEEL THAT THEY ARE
JOINED FOR LIFE — TO
BE WITH EACH OTHER IN
SILENT UNSPEAKABLE
MEMORIES.

George Eliot

THE DESIRE TO BE
AND HAVE A SISTER
IS A PRIMITIVE AND
PROFOUND ONE.

Elizabeth Fishel

MY SISTERS HAVE
TAUGHT ME HOW
TO LIVE.

George Wasserstein

SISTERS ARE
FRIENDS WE HAVE
FOR A LIFETIME.

Catherine Pulsifer

WHEN YOU LOOK AT YOUR
LIFE, THE GREATEST
HAPPINESSES ARE
FAMILY HAPPINESSES.

Joyce Brothers

A SISTER IS ONE OF THE
NICEST THINGS THAT
CAN HAPPEN TO ANYONE.

Anonymous

Meet Esme!

Our feathered friend Esme loves finding perfect
quotes for the perfect occasion, and is almost as
good at collecting them as she is at collecting twigs
for her nest. She's always full of joy and happiness,
singing her messages of goodwill in this series
of uplifting, heart-warming books.

Follow Esme on Twitter at **@EsmeTheBird**
for a daily dose of cheer!

For more information about our books,
find us on Facebook at **Summersdale Publishers**
and follow us on Twitter at **@Summersdale**.

www.summersdale.com